This planner
belongs to

_____

_____

_____

2022 AT A GLANCE

JANUARY 2022

S	M	T	W	T	F	S
						1
2	3	4	5	6	7	8
9	10	11	12	13	14	15
16	17	18	19	20	21	22
23	24	25	26	27	28	29
30	31					

FEBRUARY 2022

S	M	T	W	T	F	S
		1	2	3	4	5
6	7	8	9	10	11	12
13	14	15	16	17	18	19
20	21	22	23	24	25	26
27	28					

MARCH 2022

S	M	T	W	T	F	S
		1	2	3	4	5
6	7	8	9	10	11	12
13	14	15	16	17	18	19
20	21	22	23	24	25	26
27	28	29	30	31		

APRIL 2022

S	M	T	W	T	F	S
					1	2
3	4	5	6	7	8	9
10	11	12	13	14	15	16
17	18	19	20	21	22	23
24	25	26	27	28	29	30

MAY 2022

S	M	T	W	T	F	S
1	2	3	4	5	6	7
8	9	10	11	12	13	14
15	16	17	18	19	20	21
22	23	24	25	26	27	28
29	30	31				

JUNE 2022

S	M	T	W	T	F	S
			1	2	3	4
5	6	7	8	9	10	11
12	13	14	15	16	17	18
19	20	21	22	23	24	25
26	27	28	29	30		

JULY 2022

S	M	T	W	T	F	S
					1	2
3	4	5	6	7	8	9
10	11	12	13	14	15	16
17	18	19	20	21	22	23
24	25	26	27	28	29	30
31						

AUGUST 2022

S	M	T	W	T	F	S
	1	2	3	4	5	6
7	8	9	10	11	12	13
14	15	16	17	18	19	20
21	22	23	24	25	26	27
28	29	30	31			

SEPTEMBER 2022

S	M	T	W	T	F	S
				1	2	3
4	5	6	7	8	9	10
11	12	13	14	15	16	17
18	19	20	21	22	23	24
25	26	27	28	29	30	

OCTOBER 2022

S	M	T	W	T	F	S
						1
2	3	4	5	6	7	8
9	10	11	12	13	14	15
16	17	18	19	20	21	22
23	24	25	26	27	28	29
30	31					

NOVEMBER 2022

S	M	T	W	T	F	S
		1	2	3	4	5
6	7	8	9	10	11	12
13	14	15	16	17	18	19
20	21	22	23	24	25	26
27	28	29	30			

DECEMBER 2022

S	M	T	W	T	F	S
				1	2	3
4	5	6	7	8	9	10
11	12	13	14	15	16	17
18	19	20	21	22	23	24
25	26	27	28	29	30	31

2023 AT A GLANCE

JANUARY 2023

S	M	T	W	T	F	S
1	2	3	4	5	6	7
8	9	10	11	12	13	14
15	16	17	18	19	20	21
22	23	24	25	26	27	28
29	30	31				

FEBRUARY 2023

S	M	T	W	T	F	S
			1	2	3	4
5	6	7	8	9	10	11
12	13	14	15	16	17	18
19	20	21	22	23	24	25
26	27	28				

MARCH 2023

S	M	T	W	T	F	S
			1	2	3	4
5	6	7	8	9	10	11
12	13	14	15	16	17	18
19	20	21	22	23	24	25
26	27	28	29	30	31	

APRIL 2023

S	M	T	W	T	F	S
						1
2	3	4	5	6	7	8
9	10	11	12	13	14	15
16	17	18	19	20	21	22
23	24	25	26	27	28	29
30						

MAY 2023

S	M	T	W	T	F	S
	1	2	3	4	5	6
7	8	9	10	11	12	13
14	15	16	17	18	19	20
21	22	23	24	25	26	27
28	29	30	31			

JUNE 2023

S	M	T	W	T	F	S
				1	2	3
4	5	6	7	8	9	10
11	12	13	14	15	16	17
18	19	20	21	22	23	24
25	26	27	28	29	30	

JULY 2023

S	M	T	W	T	F	S
						1
2	3	4	5	6	7	8
9	10	11	12	13	14	15
16	17	18	19	20	21	22
23	24	25	26	27	28	29
30	31					

AUGUST 2023

S	M	T	W	T	F	S
		1	2	3	4	5
6	7	8	9	10	11	12
13	14	15	16	17	18	19
20	21	22	23	24	25	26
27	28	29	30	31		

SEPTEMBER 2023

S	M	T	W	T	F	S
					1	2
3	4	5	6	7	8	9
10	11	12	13	14	15	16
17	18	19	20	21	22	23
24	25	26	27	28	29	30

OCTOBER 2023

S	M	T	W	T	F	S
1	2	3	4	5	6	7
8	9	10	11	12	13	14
15	16	17	18	19	20	21
22	23	24	25	26	27	28
29	30	31				

NOVEMBER 2023

S	M	T	W	T	F	S
			1	2	3	4
5	6	7	8	9	10	11
12	13	14	15	16	17	18
19	20	21	22	23	24	25
26	27	28	29	30		

DECEMBER 2023

S	M	T	W	T	F	S
					1	2
3	4	5	6	7	8	9
10	11	12	13	14	15	16
17	18	19	20	21	22	23
24	25	26	27	28	29	30
31						

HOLIDAYS

The holidays listed in this calendar are accurate to the best of our knowledge and research. All times are given in Eastern Standard Time (EST), which is noted as Eastern Daylight Time (EDT) during Daylight Saving Time.

The Islamic calendar is based on lunar observation and thus may vary depending upon the sighting of the crescent moon. Dates apply to North America.

Solar and lunar eclipses are not viewable from all regions.

AUGUST 2022
1 August Bank Holiday (Scotland)
1 Civic Holiday (Canada)
1 Lughnasa
29 Summer Bank Holiday (UK)

SEPTEMBER 2022
5 Labor Day (USA, Canada)
11 Grandparents Day
11 Patriot Day
25 Rosh Hashanah begins at sunset

OCTOBER 2022
4 Yom Kippur begins at sunset
9 Sukkot begins at sunset
10 Columbus Day
10 Indigenous Peoples Day
10 Thanksgiving (Canada)
24 Diwali
30 British Summer Time ends (UK)
31 Halloween
31 Samhain

NOVEMBER 2022
6 Daylight Saving Time ends
8 Election Day
11 Remembrance Day
   (Australia, Canada, UK)
11 Veterans Day
24 Thanksgiving
27 Advent begins
30 St. Andrew's Day (Scotland)

DECEMBER 2022
18 Hanukkah begins at sunset
25 Christmas
26 Boxing Day
   (Australia, Canada, UK)
26 Kwanzaa begins
31 New Year's Eve

JANUARY 2023
1 New Year's Day
7 Christmas (Orthodox)
16 Martin Luther King Jr. Day
22 Chinese New Year (Rabbit)
26 Australia Day

FEBRUARY 2023
1 Imbolc
2 Groundhog Day
6 Waitangi Day (New Zealand)
14 Valentine's Day
15 Flag Day (Canada)
20 Presidents' Day
21 Mardi Gras
22 Ash Wednesday, Lent begins

MARCH 2023
12 Daylight Saving Time begins
17 St. Patrick's Day
19 Mother's Day (UK)
22 Ramadan begins at sunset
26 British Summer Time
   begins (UK)

APRIL 2023
1 April Fools' Day
5 Passover begins at sunset
7 Good Friday
9 Easter
10 Easter Monday
   (Australia, Canada, UK)
16 Pascha (Orthodox)
20 Eid al-Fitr begins at sunset
22 Earth Day
25 ANZAC Day
   (Australia, New Zealand)
28 Arbor Day

MAY 2023
1 Beltane
1 Early May Bank Holiday (UK)
1 May Day
5 Cinco de Mayo
5 Vesak
14 Mother's Day
22 Victoria Day (Canada)
25 Shavuot begins at sunset
29 Memorial Day
29 Spring Bank Holiday (UK)

JUNE 2023
5 World Environment Day
14 Flag Day
18 Father's Day
19 Juneteenth
27 Eid al-Adha begins at sunset

JULY 2023
1 Canada Day
4 Independence Day
12 Orangemen's Day
   (Northern Ireland)
18 Muharram begins at sunset

AUGUST 2023
1 Lughnasa
7 August Bank Holiday (Scotland)
7 Civic Holiday (Canada)
28 Summer Bank Holiday (UK)

SEPTEMBER 2023
4 Labor Day (USA, Canada)
10 Grandparents Day
11 Patriot Day
15 Rosh Hashanah begins at sunset
24 Yom Kippur begins at sunset
29 Sukkot begins at sunset

OCTOBER 2023
9 Columbus Day
9 Indigenous Peoples Day
9 Thanksgiving (Canada)
29 British Summer Time ends (UK)
31 Halloween
31 Samhain

NOVEMBER 2023
5 Daylight Saving Time ends
7 Election Day
11 Remembrance Day
   (Australia, Canada, UK)
11 Veterans Day
12 Diwali
23 Thanksgiving
30 St. Andrew's Day (Scotland)

DECEMBER 2023
3 Advent begins
7 Hanukkah begins at sunset
25 Christmas
26 Boxing Day
   (Australia, Canada, UK)
26 Kwanzaa begins
31 New Year's Eve

AUGUST 2022

SUNDAY	MONDAY	TUESDAY	WEDNESDAY
31	1	2	3
	August Bank Holiday (Scotland) Civic Holiday (Canada)		
7	8	9	10
14	15	16	17
21	22	23	24
28	29	30	31
	Summer Bank Holiday (UK)		

● NEW MOON ◑ FIRST QUARTER ○ FULL MOON ◐ LAST QUARTER

THURSDAY	FRIDAY	SATURDAY
4	◐ 7:06 am EDT 5	6
○ 9:36 pm EDT 11	12	13
18	◑ 12:36 am EDT 19	20
25	26	● 4:17 am EDT 27
1	2	3

AUGUST

August 2022

MONDAY

1

August Bank Holiday (Scotland) | Civic Holiday (Canada) | Lughnasa

TUESDAY

2

WEDNESDAY

3

FRIDAY

5

◑ 7:06 am EDT

SATURDAY

6

SUNDAY

7

AUGUST

August 2022

MONDAY

8

TUESDAY

9

WEDNESDAY

10

○ 9:36 pm EDT

AUGUST

August 2022

MONDAY
15

TUESDAY
16

WEDNESDAY
17

◑ 12:36 am EDT

AUGUST

August 2022

MONDAY
22

TUESDAY
23

WEDNESDAY
24

FRIDAY

26

Women's Equality Day

SATURDAY

27

● 4:17 am EDT

SUNDAY

28

AUGUST

August 2022

MONDAY

29

TUESDAY

30

Summer Bank Holiday (UK)

WEDNESDAY

31

SEPTEMBER 2022

SUNDAY	MONDAY	TUESDAY	WEDNESDAY
28	29	30	31
4	5	6	7
	Labor Day (USA, Canada)		
11	12	13	14
18	19	20	21
● 5:54 pm EDT 25	26	27	28
Rosh Hashanah begins at sunset			

● NEW MOON   ◐ FIRST QUARTER   ○ FULL MOON   ◑ LAST QUARTER

THURSDAY	FRIDAY	SATURDAY	
1	2	◐ 2:08 pm EDT 3	
8	9	○ 5:59 am EDT 10	
15	16	◑ 5:52 pm EDT 17	
22	23	24	
Autumnal Equinox 29	30	1	

September 2022

FRIDAY

2

SATURDAY

3

◑ 2:08 pm EDT

SUNDAY

4

September 2022

MONDAY

5

Labor Day (USA, Canada)

TUESDAY

6

WEDNESDAY

7

8

9

Mercury Retrograde until October 2

10

○ 5:59 am EDT

11

Grandparents Day | Patriot Day

September 2022

MONDAY

12

TUESDAY

13

WEDNESDAY

14

FRIDAY
16

SATURDAY
17

◑ 5:52 pm EDT

SUNDAY
18

September 2022

MONDAY
19

TUESDAY
20

WEDNESDAY
21

International Day of Peace

THURSDAY
22

Autumnal Equinox 9:04 pm EDT

FRIDAY
23

SATURDAY
24

SUNDAY
25

Rosh Hashanah begins at sunset | ● 5:54 pm EDT

September 2022

MONDAY
26

TUESDAY
27

WEDNESDAY
28

THURSDAY

29

SEPTEMBER

FRIDAY

30

OCTOBER 2022

SUNDAY	MONDAY	TUESDAY	WEDNESDAY
25	26	27	28
◗ 8:14 pm EDT 2	3	4	5
		Yom Kippur begins at sunset	
○ 4:55 pm EDT 9	10	11	12
	Columbus Day Indigenous Peoples Day Thanksgiving (Canada)		
16	◑ 1:15 pm EDT 17	18	19
23	24	● 6:49 am EDT 25	26
30 British Summer Time ends (UK)	31 Halloween		

● NEW MOON   ◑ FIRST QUARTER   ○ FULL MOON   ◗ LAST QUARTER

THURSDAY	FRIDAY	SATURDAY
29	30	1
6	7	8
13	14	15
20	21	22
27	28	29

OCTOBER

October 2022

SATURDAY
1

SUNDAY
2

◑ 8:14 pm EDT

October 2022

MONDAY

3

TUESDAY

4

Yom Kippur begins at sunset

WEDNESDAY

5

6

7

OCTOBER

8

9

Sukkot begins at sunset | ○ 4:55 pm EDT

October 2022

MONDAY

10

Columbus Day | Indigenous Peoples Day | Thanksgiving (Canada)

TUESDAY

11

WEDNESDAY

12

OCTOBER

October 2022

MONDAY

17

◐ 1:15 pm EDT

TUESDAY

18

WEDNESDAY

19

THURSDAY

20

FRIDAY

21

OCTOBER

SATURDAY

22

SUNDAY

23

October 2022

MONDAY

24

Diwali | United Nations Day

TUESDAY

25

Partial Solar Eclipse 7:00 am EDT | ● 6:49 am EDT

WEDNESDAY

26

THURSDAY
27

FRIDAY
28

OCTOBER

SATURDAY
29

SUNDAY
30

British Summer Time ends (UK)

October 2022

MONDAY
31

Halloween | Samhain

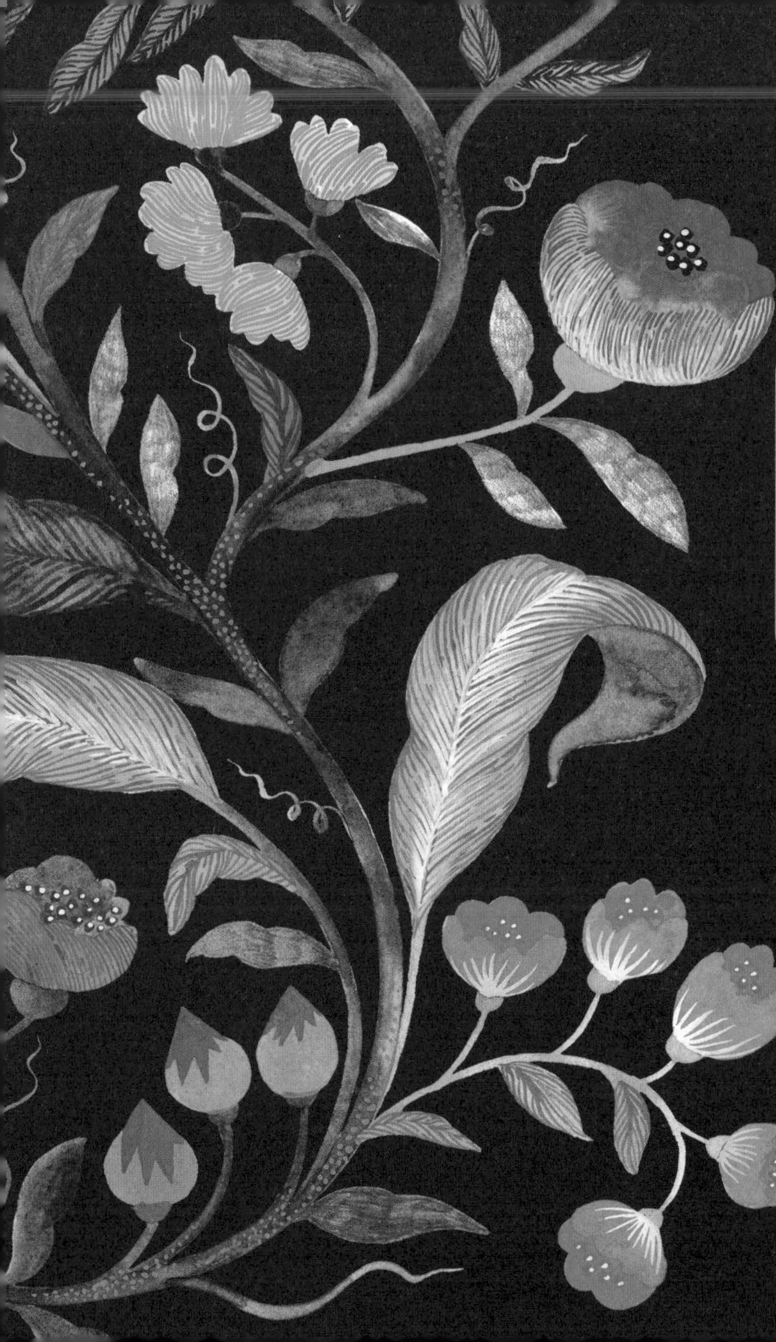

OCTOBER

NOVEMBER 2022

SUNDAY	MONDAY	TUESDAY	WEDNESDAY
30	31	◑ 2:37 am EDT 1	2
6	7	○ 6:02 am EST 8	9
Daylight Saving Time ends		Election Day	
13	14	15	◑ 8:27 am EST 16
20	21	22	● 5:57 pm EST 23
27	28	29	◑ 9:36 am EST 30
			St. Andrew's Day (Scotland)

 ● NEW MOON ◐ FIRST QUARTER ○ FULL MOON ◑ LAST QUARTER

THURSDAY	FRIDAY	SATURDAY
3	4	5
10	11	12
	Remembrance Day (Australia, Canada, UK) Veterans Day	
17	18	19
24	25	26
Thanksgiving		
1	2	3

November 2022

TUESDAY

1

◗ 2:37 am EDT

WEDNESDAY

2

THURSDAY

3

FRIDAY

4

SATURDAY

5

NOVEMBER

SUNDAY

6

Daylight Saving Time ends

November 2022

MONDAY

7

TUESDAY

8

Election Day | Total Lunar Eclipse 5:59 am EST | ○ 6:02 am EST

WEDNESDAY

9

10

11

Remembrance Day (Australia, Canada, UK) | Veterans Day

12

NOVEMBER

13

November 2022

MONDAY

14

TUESDAY

15

WEDNESDAY

16

◑ 8:27 am EST

THURSDAY

17

FRIDAY

18

SATURDAY

19

SUNDAY

20

November 2022

MONDAY
21

TUESDAY
22

WEDNESDAY
23

● 5:57 pm EST

24

Thanksgiving

25

26

NOVEMBER

27

Advent begins

November 2022

MONDAY

28

TUESDAY

29

WEDNESDAY

30

St. Andrew's Day (Scotland) | ◑ 9:36 am EST

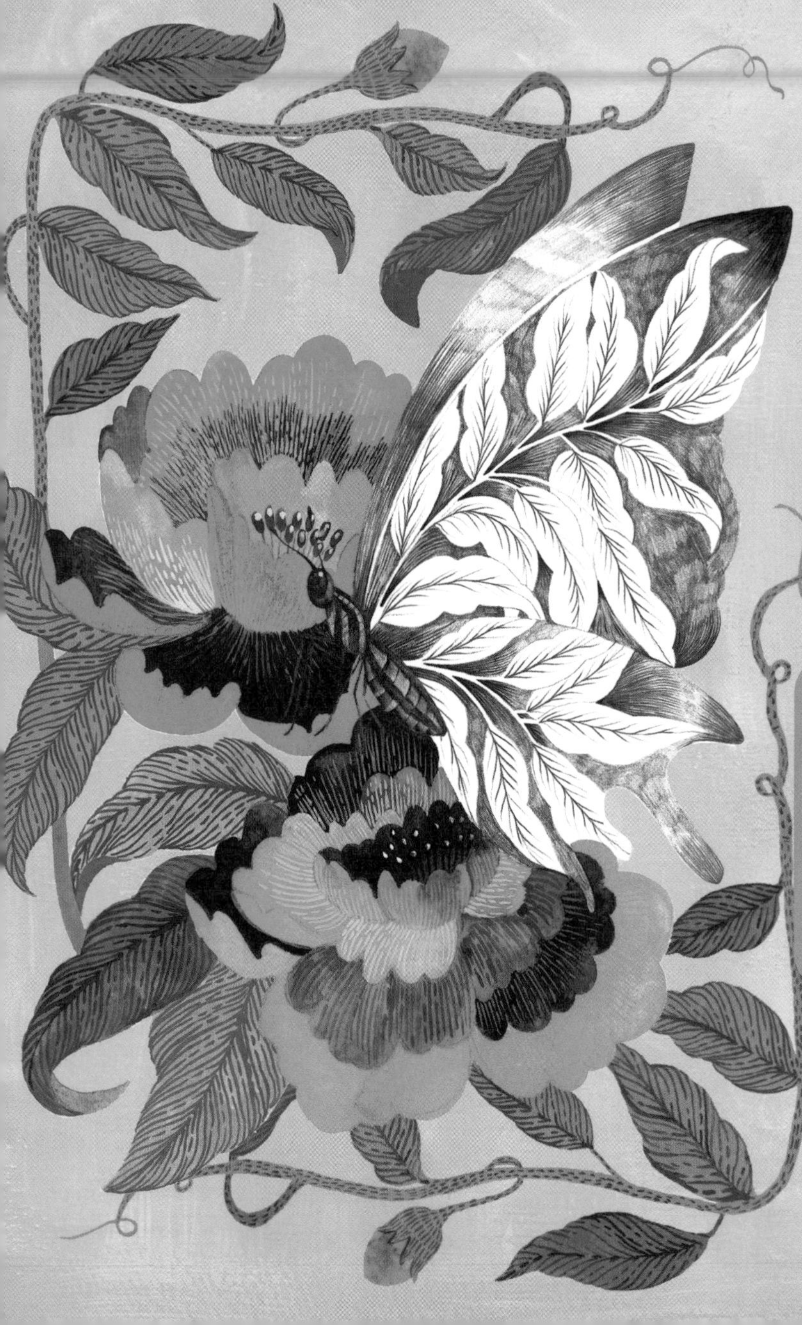

NOVEMBER

DECEMBER 2022

SUNDAY	MONDAY	TUESDAY	WEDNESDAY
27	28	29	30
4	5	6	○ 11:08 pm EST 7
11	12	13	14
18	19	20	21 Winter Solstice
25 Christmas Hanukkah begins at sunset	26 Boxing Day (Australia, Canada, UK) Kwanzaa begins	27	28

● NEW MOON ◐ FIRST QUARTER ○ FULL MOON ◑ LAST QUARTER

THURSDAY	FRIDAY	SATURDAY
1	2	3
8	9	10
15	◑ 3:56 am EST 16	17
22	● 5:17 am EST 23	24
◑ 8:20 pm EST 29	30	31
		New Year's Eve

December 2022

THURSDAY

1

FRIDAY

2

SATURDAY

3

SUNDAY

4

DECEMBER

December 2022

MONDAY

5

TUESDAY

6

WEDNESDAY

7

Pearl Harbor Remembrance Day | ○ 11:08 pm EST

THURSDAY

8

FRIDAY

9

SATURDAY

10

Human Rights Day

SUNDAY

11

December 2022

MONDAY
12

TUESDAY
13

WEDNESDAY
14

THURSDAY

15

FRIDAY

16

◗ 3:56 am EST

SATURDAY

17

SUNDAY

18

Hanukkah begins at sunset

DECEMBER

December 2022

MONDAY

19

TUESDAY

20

WEDNESDAY

21

Winter Solstice 4:48 pm EST

THURSDAY

22

FRIDAY

23

● 5:17 am EST

SATURDAY

24

SUNDAY

25

Christmas

DECEMBER

December 2022

MONDAY

26

Boxing Day (Australia, Canada, UK) | Kwanzaa begins

TUESDAY

27

WEDNESDAY

28

Mercury Retrograde until January 18 | ◐ 8:20 pm EST

AM: 103/73

New Year's Eve

DECEMBER

JANUARY 2023

SUNDAY	MONDAY	TUESDAY	WEDNESDAY
1 New Year's Day	2	3	4
8	9	10	11
15	16 Martin Luther King Jr. Day	17	18
22	23	24	25
29	30	31	1

● NEW MOON   ◐ FIRST QUARTER   ○ FULL MOON   ◑ LAST QUARTER

THURSDAY	FRIDAY	SATURDAY
5	○ 6:08 pm EST 6	7
12	13	◐ 9:10 pm EST 14
19	20	● 3:53 pm EST 21
26	27	◑ 10:19 am EST 28
Australia Day 2	3	4

January 2023

SUNDAY

1

New Year's Day

January 2023

MONDAY

2

TUESDAY

3

WEDNESDAY

4

THURSDAY

5

FRIDAY

6

○ 6:08 pm EST

SATURDAY

7

Christmas (Orthodox Christian)

SUNDAY

8

January 2023

MONDAY

9

TUESDAY

10

WEDNESDAY

11

FRIDAY

13

SATURDAY

14

◖ 9:10 pm EST

SUNDAY

15

January *2023*

MONDAY
16

Martin Luther King Jr. Day

TUESDAY
17

WEDNESDAY
18

THURSDAY

19

FRIDAY

20

SATURDAY

21

● 3:53 pm EST

SUNDAY

22

Chinese New Year (Rabbit)

January 2023

MONDAY
23

TUESDAY
24

WEDNESDAY
25

Australia Day

◑ 10:19 am EST

January 2023

MONDAY
30

TUESDAY
31

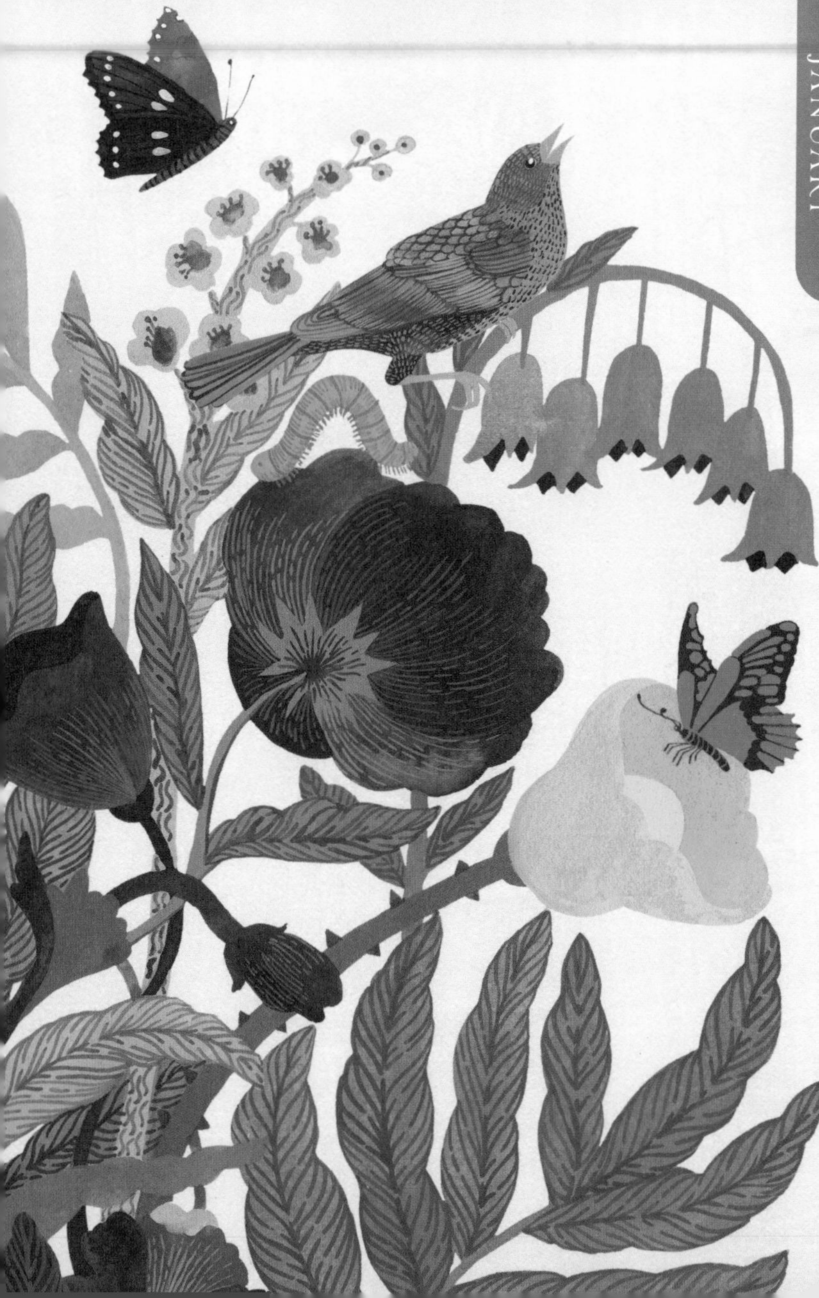

FEBRUARY 2023

SUNDAY	MONDAY	TUESDAY	WEDNESDAY
29	30	31	1
○ 1:29 pm EST 5	6	7	8
12	◑ 11:01 am EST 13	14 Valentine's Day	15 Flag Day (Canada)
19	● 2:06 am EST 20 Presidents' Day	21	22 Ash Wednesday, Lent begins
26	◐ 3:06 am EST 27	28	1

THURSDAY	FRIDAY	SATURDAY
2	3	4
Groundhog Day		
9	10	11
16	17	18
23	24	25
2	3	4

February 2023

WEDNESDAY

1

Imbolc

Groundhog Day

○ 1:29 pm EST

February 2023

MONDAY

6

Waitangi Day (New Zealand)

TUESDAY

7

WEDNESDAY

8

Lincoln's Birthday

February *2023*

MONDAY

13

◗ 11:01 am EST

TUESDAY

14

Valentine's Day

WEDNESDAY

15

Flag Day (Canada)

THURSDAY

16

FRIDAY

17

FEBRUARY

Random Acts of Kindness Day

SATURDAY

18

SUNDAY

19

February 2023

MONDAY

20

Presidents' Day | ● 2:06 am EST

TUESDAY

21

Mardi Gras

WEDNESDAY

22

Ash Wednesday, Lent begins | Washington's Birthday

23

24

FEBRUARY

25

26

February 2023

MONDAY
27

◐ 3:06 am EST
TUESDAY
28

MARCH 2023

SUNDAY	MONDAY	TUESDAY	WEDNESDAY
26	27	28	1
5	6	○ 7:40 am EST 7	8
12	13	◐ 10:08 pm EDT 14	15
19 Daylight Saving Time begins	20 Spring Equinox	● 1:23 pm EDT 21	22 Ramadan begins at sunset
26 British Summer Time begins (UK)	27	◑ 10:32 pm EDT 28	29

 ● NEW MOON ◐ FIRST QUARTER ○ FULL MOON ◑ LAST QUARTER

THURSDAY	FRIDAY	SATURDAY	
2	3	4	
9	10	11	
16	17	18	
	St. Patrick's Day		
23	24	25	
30	31	1	

MARCH

March 2023

WEDNESDAY

1

MARCH

March 2023

MONDAY

6

TUESDAY

7

○ 7:40 am EST

WEDNESDAY

8

International Women's Day

FRIDAY

10

SATURDAY

11

MARCH

SUNDAY

12

Daylight Saving Time begins

March 2023

MONDAY
13

TUESDAY
14

◑ 10:08 pm EDT

WEDNESDAY
15

16

17

St. Patrick's Day

18

MARCH

19

Mother's Day (UK)

March 2023

MONDAY

20

Spring Equinox 5:25 pm EDT

TUESDAY

21

● 1:23 pm EDT

WEDNESDAY

22

Ramadan begins at sunset

23

24

25

MARCH

26

British Summer Time begins (UK)

March 2023

MONDAY

27

TUESDAY

28

◑ 10:32 pm EDT

WEDNESDAY

29

APRIL 2023

SUNDAY	MONDAY	TUESDAY	WEDNESDAY
26	27	28	29
2	3	4	5 Passover begins at sunset
9 Easter	10 Easter Monday (Australia, Canada, UK)	11	12
16	17	18	19
23 30	24	25 ANZAC Day (Australia, New Zealand)	26

● NEW MOON   ◐ FIRST QUARTER   ○ FULL MOON   ◑ LAST QUARTER

	30	31	1
			April Fools' Day
○ 12:34 am EDT	6	7	8
		Good Friday	
◑ 5:11 am EDT	13	14	15
● 12:12 am EDT	20	21	22
Eid al-Fitr begins at sunset			Earth Day
◐ 5:20 pm EDT	27	28	29

APRIL

April 2023

SATURDAY

1

April Fools' Day

SUNDAY

2

April 2023

MONDAY

3

TUESDAY

4

WEDNESDAY

5

Passover begins at sunset

6

○ 12:34 am EDT

7

Good Friday

8

9

APRIL

Easter

April 2023

MONDAY

10

Easter Monday (Australia, Canada, UK)

TUESDAY

11

WEDNESDAY

12

THURSDAY

13

◐ 5:11 am EDT

FRIDAY

14

SATURDAY

15

SUNDAY

16

APRIL

Pascha (Orthodox Christian)

April 2023

MONDAY

17

TUESDAY

18

Tax Day

WEDNESDAY

19

20

Eid al-Fitr begins at sunset | Hybrid Solar Eclipse 12:17 am EDT | ● 12:12 am EDT

21

Mercury Retrograde until May 14

22

Earth Day

23

APRIL

April 2023

MONDAY

24

TUESDAY

25

ANZAC Day (Australia, New Zealand)

WEDNESDAY

26

27

◗ 5:20 pm EDT

28

Arbor Day

29

30

APRIL

MAY 2023

SUNDAY	MONDAY	TUESDAY	WEDNESDAY
30	1 Early May Bank Holiday (UK)	2	3
7	8	9	10
14 Mother's Day	15	16	17
21	22 Victoria Day (Canada)	23	24
28	29 Memorial Day Spring Bank Holiday (UK)	30	31

 ● NEW MOON ◐ FIRST QUARTER ○ FULL MOON ◑ LAST QUARTER

THURSDAY	FRIDAY	SATURDAY
4	○ 1:34 pm EDT 5	6
11	◑ 10:28 am EDT 12	13
18	● 11:53 am EDT 19	20
25	26	◑ 11:22 am EDT 27
1	2	3

May 2023

MONDAY

1

Beltane | Early May Bank Holiday (UK) | May Day

TUESDAY

2

WEDNESDAY

3

THURSDAY

4

FRIDAY

5

Cinco de Mayo | Vesak | Penumbral Lunar Eclipse 1:23 pm EDT | ○ 1:34 pm EDT

SATURDAY

6

SUNDAY

7

MONDAY

8

TUESDAY

9

WEDNESDAY

10

THURSDAY
11

MAY

FRIDAY
12

◑ 10:28 am EDT

SATURDAY
13

SUNDAY
14

Mother's Day

May 2023

MONDAY
15

TUESDAY
16

WEDNESDAY
17

18

19

Bike to Work Day | ● 11:53 am EDT

20

Armed Forces Day

21

May 2023

MONDAY

22

Victoria Day (Canada)

TUESDAY

23

WEDNESDAY

24

25

Shavuot begins at sunset

26

27

◗ 11:22 am EDT

28

May 2023

MONDAY

29

Memorial Day | Spring Bank Holiday (UK)

TUESDAY

30

WEDNESDAY

31

JUNE 2023

SUNDAY	MONDAY	TUESDAY	WEDNESDAY
28	29	30	31
4	5	6	7
11	12	13	14
● 12:37 am EDT 18	19	20	Flag Day 21
Father's Day 25	Juneteenth ◐ 3:50 am EDT 26	27	Summer Solstice 28

Eid al-Adha begins at sunset

● NEW MOON   ◐ FIRST QUARTER   ○ FULL MOON   ◑ LAST QUARTER

1	2	○ 11:42 pm EDT 3
8	9	◑ 3:31 pm EDT 10
15	16	17
22	23	24
29	30	1

JUNE

June 2023

1

2

JUNE

3

○ 11:42 pm EDT

4

June 2023

MONDAY

5

World Environment Day

TUESDAY

6

WEDNESDAY

7

FRIDAY

9

SATURDAY

10

◑ 3:31 pm EDT

SUNDAY

11

June 2023

MONDAY
12

TUESDAY
13

WEDNESDAY
14

Flag Day

15

16

JUNE

17

18

Father's Day | ● 12:37 am EDT

June 2023

MONDAY

19

Juneteenth

TUESDAY

20

World Refugee Day

WEDNESDAY

21

Summer Solstice 10:58 am EDT

THURSDAY

22

FRIDAY

23

JUNE

SATURDAY

24

SUNDAY

25

June 2023

MONDAY

26

◑ 3:50 am EDT

TUESDAY

27

Eid al-Adha begins at sunset

WEDNESDAY

28

JULY 2023

SUNDAY	MONDAY	TUESDAY	WEDNESDAY
25	26	27	28
2	○ 7:39 am EDT 3	4 Independence Day	5
◑ 9:48 pm EDT 9	10	11	12
16	● 2:32 pm EDT 17	18	19 Orangemen's Day (Northern Ireland)
23	24	◑ 6:07 pm EDT 25 Muharram begins at sunset	26
30	31		

● NEW MOON   ◑ FIRST QUARTER   ○ FULL MOON   ◑ LAST QUARTER

THURSDAY	FRIDAY	SATURDAY
29	30	1
		Canada Day
6	7	8
13	14	15
20	21	22
27	28	29

JULY

July *2023*

SATURDAY

1

Canada Day

SUNDAY

2

July 2023

○ 7:39 am EDT

Independence Day

THURSDAY

6

FRIDAY

7

SATURDAY

8

JULY

SUNDAY

9

◑ 9:48 pm EDT

July 2023

. . . .

MONDAY

10

. . . .

TUESDAY

11

. . . .

WEDNESDAY

12

Orangemen's Day (Northern Ireland)

. . . .

THURSDAY
13

FRIDAY
14

SATURDAY
15

JULY

SUNDAY
16

July 2023

MONDAY
17

● 2:32 pm EDT

TUESDAY
18

Muharram begins at sunset

WEDNESDAY
19

THURSDAY

20

FRIDAY

21

SATURDAY

22

JULY

SUNDAY

23

July 2023

◑ 6:07 pm EDT

THURSDAY
27

FRIDAY
28

SATURDAY
29

SUNDAY
30

July 2023

JULY

AUGUST 2023

SUNDAY	MONDAY	TUESDAY	WEDNESDAY
30	31	○ 2:31 pm EDT 1	2
6	7	◑ 6:28 am EDT 8	9
	August Bank Holiday (Scotland) Civic Holiday (Canada)		
13	14	15	● 5:38 am EDT 16
20	21	22	23
27	28	29	○ 9:35 pm EDT (Blue Moon) 30
	Summer Bank Holiday (UK)		

● NEW MOON   ◐ FIRST QUARTER   ○ FULL MOON   ◑ LAST QUARTER

THURSDAY	FRIDAY	SATURDAY
3	4	5
10	11	12
17	18	19
☽ 5:57 am EDT 24	25	26
31	1	2

AUGUST

August 2023

TUESDAY

1

Lughnasa | ○ 2:31 pm EDT

WEDNESDAY

2

THURSDAY

3

FRIDAY

4

SATURDAY

5

SUNDAY

6

August 2023

MONDAY

7

August Bank Holiday (Scotland) | Civic Holiday (Canada)

TUESDAY

8

◑ 6:28 am EDT

WEDNESDAY

9

AUGUST

August 2023

MONDAY

14

TUESDAY

15

WEDNESDAY

16

● 5:38 am EDT

THURSDAY
17

FRIDAY
18

SATURDAY
19

SUNDAY
20

August 2023

MONDAY

21

TUESDAY

22

WEDNESDAY

23

Mercury Retrograde until September 15

24

◑ 5:57 am EDT

25

26

Women's Equality Day

27

AUGUST

August 2023

MONDAY
28

Summer Bank Holiday (UK)

TUESDAY
29

WEDNESDAY
30

○ 9:35 pm EDT (Blue Moon)

SEPTEMBER 2023

SUNDAY	MONDAY	TUESDAY	WEDNESDAY
27	28	29	30
3	4	5	◑ 6:21 pm EDT 6
	Labor Day (USA, Canada)		
10	11	12	13
17	18	19	20
24	25	26	27
Yom Kippur begins at sunset			

● NEW MOON ◐ FIRST QUARTER ○ FULL MOON ◑ LAST QUARTER

THURSDAY	FRIDAY	SATURDAY
31	1	2
7	8	9
● 9:40 pm EDT 14	15	16
	Rosh Hashanah begins at sunset	
21	◑ 3:32 pm EDT 22	23
		Autumnal Equinox
28	○ 5:57 am EDT 29	30

September 2023

FRIDAY
1

SATURDAY
2

SUNDAY
3

September 2023

MONDAY

4

Labor Day (USA, Canada)

TUESDAY

5

WEDNESDAY

6

◑ 6:21 pm EDT

THURSDAY
7

FRIDAY
8

SATURDAY
9

SUNDAY
10

Grandparents Day

September 2023

MONDAY

11

Patriot Day

TUESDAY

12

WEDNESDAY

13

● 9:40 pm EDT

Rosh Hashanah begins at sunset

September 2023

MONDAY

18

TUESDAY

19

WEDNESDAY

20

21

International Day of Peace

22

◑ 3:32 pm EDT

23

Autumnal Equinox 2:50 am EDT

24

Yom Kippur begins at sunset

September 2023

MONDAY
25

TUESDAY
26

WEDNESDAY
27

Sukkot begins at sunset | ○ 5:57 am EDT

OCTOBER 2023

SUNDAY	MONDAY	TUESDAY	WEDNESDAY
1	2	3	4
8	9	10	11
	Columbus Day Indigenous Peoples Day Thanksgiving (Canada)		
15	16	17	18
22	23	24	25
29	30	31	1
British Summer Time ends (UK)		Halloween	

● NEW MOON   ◐ FIRST QUARTER   ○ FULL MOON   ◑ LAST QUARTER

THURSDAY	FRIDAY	SATURDAY
5	◐ 9:48 am EDT 6	7
12	13	● 1:55 pm EDT 14
19	20	◐ 11:29 pm EDT 21
26	27	○ 4:24 pm EDT 28
2	3	4

OCTOBER

October 2023

SUNDAY

1

October 2023

MONDAY

2

TUESDAY

3

WEDNESDAY

4

THURSDAY

5

FRIDAY

6

OCTOBER

◑ 9:48 am EDT

SATURDAY

7

SUNDAY

8

October 2023

MONDAY

9

Columbus Day | Indigenous Peoples Day | Thanksgiving (Canada)

TUESDAY

10

WEDNESDAY

11

OCTOBER

Annular Solar Eclipse 1:59 pm EDT | ● 1:55 pm EDT

October 2023

MONDAY

16

TUESDAY

17

WEDNESDAY

18

19

20

OCTOBER

21

◑ 11:29 pm EDT

22

October 2023

MONDAY

23

TUESDAY

24

United Nations Day

WEDNESDAY

25

OCTOBER

Partial Lunar Eclipse 4:14 pm EDT | ○ 4:24 pm EDT

British Summer Time ends (UK)

October 2023

MONDAY
30

TUESDAY
31

Halloween | Samhain

NOVEMBER 2023

SUNDAY	MONDAY	TUESDAY	WEDNESDAY
29	30	31	1
◑ 3:37 am EST 5	6	7	8
Daylight Saving Time ends 12	● 4:27 am EST 13	Election Day 14	15
19	◐ 5:50 am EST 20	21	22
26	○ 4:16 am EST 27	28	29

 ● NEW MOON ◐ FIRST QUARTER ○ FULL MOON ◑ LAST QUARTER

THURSDAY	FRIDAY	SATURDAY
2	3	4
9	10	11 Remembrance Day (Australia, Canada, UK) Veterans Day
16	17	18
23	24	25
Thanksgiving		
30	1	2
St. Andrew's Day (Scotland)		

NOVEMBER

November 2023

WEDNESDAY

1

NOVEMBER

Daylight Saving Time ends | ◑ 3:37 am EST

November 2023

MONDAY

6

TUESDAY

7

Election Day

WEDNESDAY

8

9

10

11

Remembrance Day (Australia, Canada, UK) | Veterans Day

12

Diwali

NOVEMBER

November 2023

MONDAY

13

● 4:27 am EST

TUESDAY

14

WEDNESDAY

15

NOVEMBER

November 2023

MONDAY

20

◐ 5:50 am EST

TUESDAY

21

WEDNESDAY

22

THURSDAY

23

Thanksgiving

FRIDAY

24

SATURDAY

25

NOVEMBER

SUNDAY

26

November 2023

MONDAY

27

○ 4:16 am EST

TUESDAY

28

WEDNESDAY

29

St. Andrew's Day (Scotland)

NOVEMBER

DECEMBER 2023

SUNDAY	MONDAY	TUESDAY	WEDNESDAY
26	27	28	29
3	4	◑ 12:49 am EST 5	6
10	11	● 6:32 pm EST 12	13
17	18	◑ 1:39 pm EST 19	20
24	25	○ 7:33 pm EST 26	27
31			
New Year's Eve	Christmas	Boxing Day (Australia, Canada, UK) Kwanzaa begins	

● NEW MOON ◑ FIRST QUARTER ○ FULL MOON ◐ LAST QUARTER

THURSDAY	FRIDAY	SATURDAY	
30	1	2	
7	8	9	
Hanukkah begins at sunset			
14	15	16	
21	22	23	
Winter Solstice			
28	29	30	

DECEMBER

December 2023

FRIDAY
1

SATURDAY
2

SUNDAY
3

Advent begins

December 2023

MONDAY

4

TUESDAY

5

◑ 12:49 am EST

WEDNESDAY

6

Hanukkah begins at sunset | Pearl Harbor Remembrance Day

Human Rights Day

December 2023

MONDAY

11

TUESDAY

12

● 6:32 pm EST

WEDNESDAY

13

Mercury Retrograde until January 1

14

15

16

17

December 2023

MONDAY

18

TUESDAY

19

◑ 1:39 pm EST

WEDNESDAY

20

21

Winter Solstice 10:28 pm EST

22

23

24

DECEMBER

December 2023

MONDAY

25

Christmas

TUESDAY

26

Boxing Day (Australia, Canada, UK) | Kwanzaa begins | ○ 7:33 pm EST

WEDNESDAY

27

THURSDAY
28

FRIDAY
29

SATURDAY
30

SUNDAY
31

New Year's Eve

JANUARY 2024

SUNDAY	MONDAY	TUESDAY	WEDNESDAY
31	1	2	◐ 10:30 pm EST 3
	New Year's Day		
7	8	9	10
14	15	16	◑ 10:53 pm EST 17
	Martin Luther King Jr. Day		
21	22	23	24
28	29	30	31

● NEW MOON ◑ FIRST QUARTER ○ FULL MOON ◐ LAST QUARTER

THURSDAY	FRIDAY	SATURDAY
4	5	6
● 6:57 am EST 11	12	13
18	19	20
○ 12:54 pm EST 25	26	27
1	2 Australia Day	3

BIRTHDAYS & OCCASIONS

JANUARY

FEBRUARY

MARCH

APRIL

MAY

JUNE

BIRTHDAYS & OCCASIONS

JLY

AUGUST

EPTEMBER

OCTOBER

OVEMBER

DECEMBER

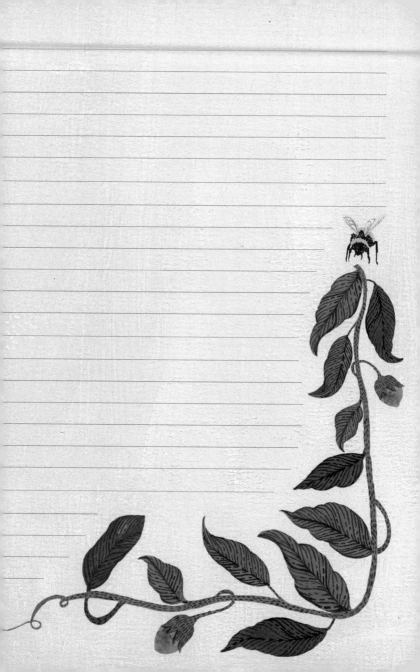

2024 AT A GLANCE

JANUARY 2024

S	M	T	W	T	F	S
	1	2	3	4	5	6
7	8	9	10	11	12	13
14	15	16	17	18	19	20
21	22	23	24	25	26	27
28	29	30	31			

FEBRUARY 2024

S	M	T	W	T	F	S
				1	2	3
4	5	6	7	8	9	10
11	12	13	14	15	16	17
18	19	20	21	22	23	24
25	26	27	28	29		

MARCH 2024

S	M	T	W	T	F	S
					1	2
3	4	5	6	7	8	9
10	11	12	13	14	15	16
17	18	19	20	21	22	23
24	25	26	27	28	29	30
31						

APRIL 2024

S	M	T	W	T	F	S
	1	2	3	4	5	6
7	8	9	10	11	12	13
14	15	16	17	18	19	20
21	22	23	24	25	26	27
28	29	30				

MAY 2024

S	M	T	W	T	F	S
			1	2	3	4
5	6	7	8	9	10	11
12	13	14	15	16	17	18
19	20	21	22	23	24	25
26	27	28	29	30	31	

JUNE 2024

S	M	T	W	T	F	S
						1
2	3	4	5	6	7	8
9	10	11	12	13	14	15
16	17	18	19	20	21	22
23	24	25	26	27	28	29
30						

JULY 2024

S	M	T	W	T	F	S
	1	2	3	4	5	6
7	8	9	10	11	12	13
14	15	16	17	18	19	20
21	22	23	24	25	26	27
28	29	30	31			

AUGUST 2024

S	M	T	W	T	F	S
				1	2	3
4	5	6	7	8	9	10
11	12	13	14	15	16	17
18	19	20	21	22	23	24
25	26	27	28	29	30	31

SEPTEMBER 2024

S	M	T	W	T	F	S
1	2	3	4	5	6	7
8	9	10	11	12	13	14
15	16	17	18	19	20	21
22	23	24	25	26	27	28
29	30					

OCTOBER 2024

S	M	T	W	T	F	S
		1	2	3	4	5
6	7	8	9	10	11	12
13	14	15	16	17	18	19
20	21	22	23	24	25	26
27	28	29	30	31		

NOVEMBER 2024

S	M	T	W	T	F	S
					1	2
3	4	5	6	7	8	9
10	11	12	13	14	15	16
17	18	19	20	21	22	23
24	25	26	27	28	29	30

DECEMBER 2024

S	M	T	W	T	F	S
1	2	3	4	5	6	7
8	9	10	11	12	13	14
15	16	17	18	19	20	21
22	23	24	25	26	27	28
29	30	31				